PIANO · VOCAL · GUITAR

Gnomeo & Juliet

MUSIC FROM THE MOTION PICTURE SOUNDTRACK

ISBN 978-1-4584-0240-0

WALT DISNEY MUSIC COMPANY
WONDERLAND MUSIC COMPANY, INC.

DISTRIBUTED BY

HAL•LEONARD®
CORPORATION

7777 W. BLUEMOUND RD. P.O. BOX 13819 MILWAUKEE, WI 53213

Visit Hal Leonard Online at
www.halleonard.com

HELLO HELLO

Music by ELTON JOHN
Lyrics by BERNIE TAUPIN

Feel of feel-ing liked. Head-ed out to see the sights. Ain't
"Nev-er gon-na find an-y-thing to change my mind."
Do a diz-zy dance. Twirl a-round and take a chance. Noth-in's

life a man-y-splen-dored thing? _____
Fam-ous last lines of the fool. _____
eas-y; noth-in' comes for free. _____

CROCODILE ROCK

Words and Music by ELTON JOHN
and BERNIE TAUPIN

Moderately fast

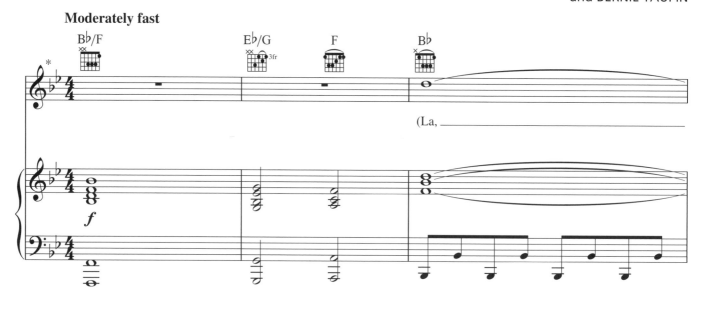

(La, _____

la, la, la, la, la, _____ la, la, la, la

la, _____ la, la, la, la, la.) _____

* Recorded a half step higher.

SATURDAY NIGHT'S ALRIGHT
(For Fighting)

Words and Music by ELTON JOHN
and BERNIE TAUPIN

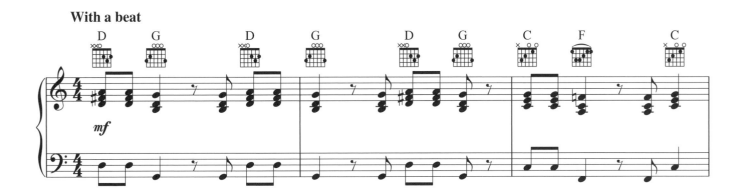

With a beat

(2nd time) It's   get - ting late. __   Have you   seen   my   mates? __   Ma,

packed   pret - ty   tight   in   here   to - night. __   I'm

tell   me   when   the   boys   get   here. _____   It's   sev - en   o' - clock __   and   I

look - ing   for   a   dol - ly   to _____ see   me   right.   I   may   use   a   lit - tle   mus - cle   to

DON'T GO BREAKING MY HEART

Words and Music by CARTE BLANCHE
and ANN ORSON

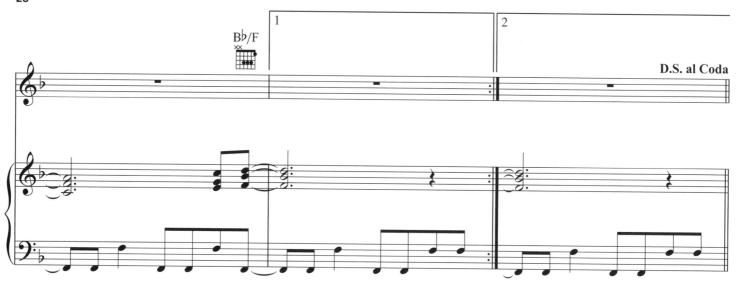

D.S. al Coda

CODA

Both:
_____ Don't go break-ing my, don't go break-ing my, don't go break-ing my heart. _____

Female:
I won't go break-ing your heart. _____ don't go break-ing my heart. _____

LOVE BUILDS A GARDEN

Music by ELTON JOHN
Lyrics by BERNIE TAUPIN

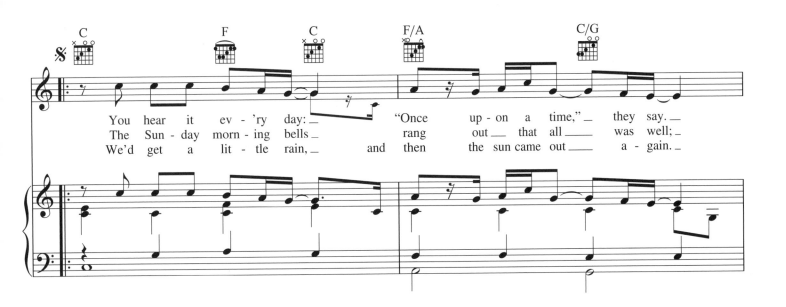

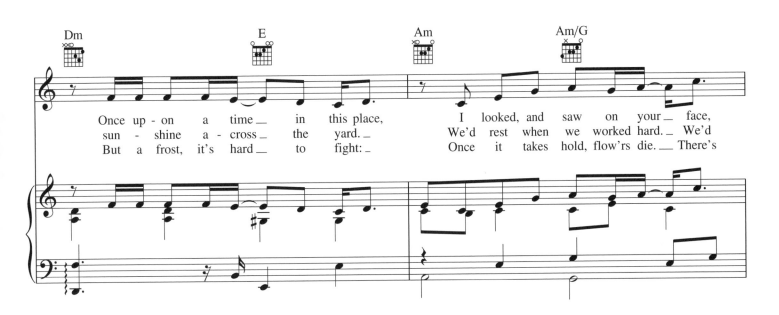

YOUR SONG

Words and Music by ELTON JOHN
and BERNIE TAUPIN

Slow, but with a beat

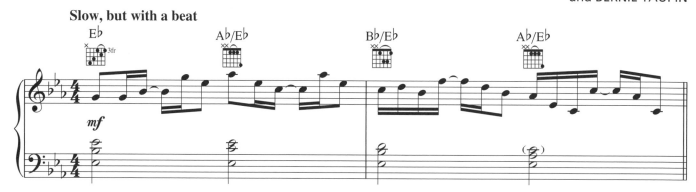

It's a lit-tle bit fun-ny _____ this feel - ing in - side, _____
If I was a sculp-tor, _____ but then _____ a-gain no, _____ or a
I sat on the roof _____ and kicked _____ off the moss, _____ well a
So ex-cuse me for - get - ting, _____ but these _____ things I do. _____

man who makes po - tions in a trav-el - in' show. _____ I
few of the vers - es, well, they've got me _____ quite cross. _____
You see I've for - got - ten if _____ they're green or _____ they're blue. _____

I'm not one of those _____ who _____ can eas - i - ly hide, _____

And you ___ can tell ev - 'ry - bod - y

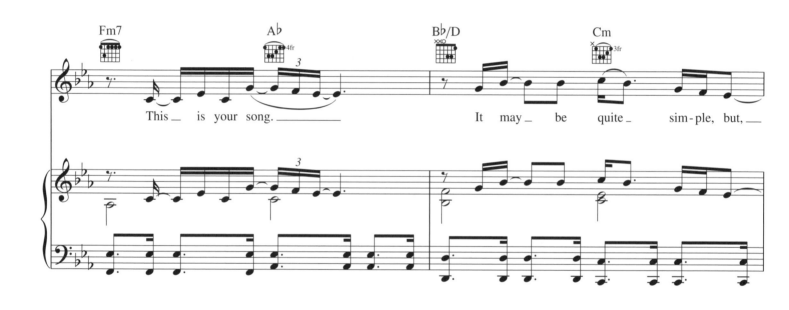

This ___ is your song. _____ It may ___ be quite ___ sim - ple, but, ___

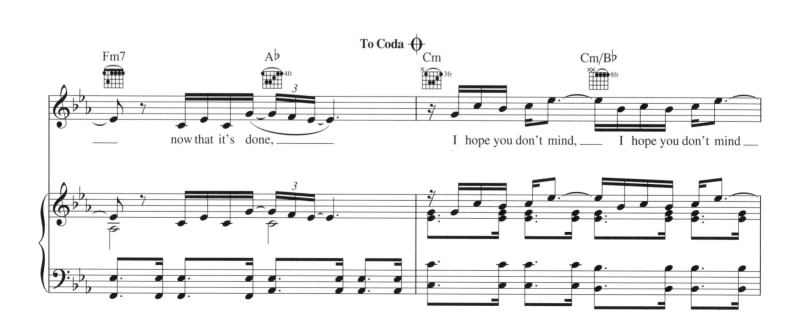

___ now that it's done, _____ I hope you don't mind, ___ I hope you don't mind ___

To Coda ⊕

that I put down in words how won-der-ful life is while

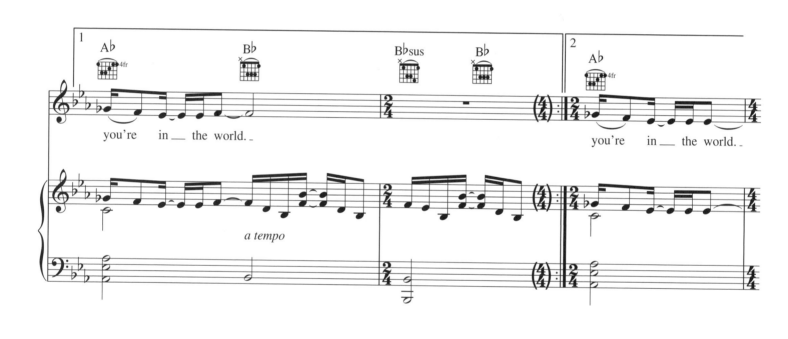

you're in the world.

a tempo

you're in the world.

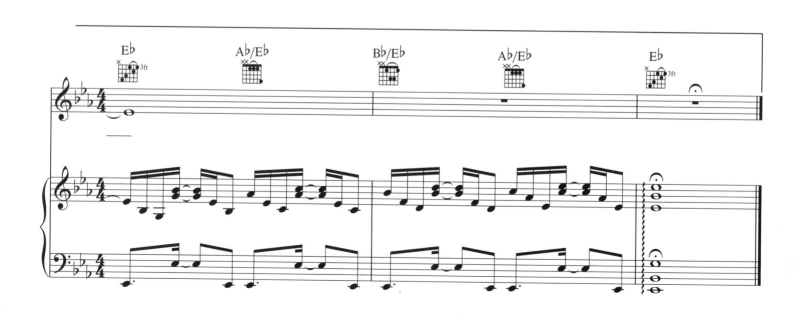

ROCKET MAN
(I Think It's Gonna Be a Long Long Time)

Words and Music by ELTON JOHN
and BERNIE TAUPIN

Moderate Ballad

She packed_ my bags_ last night pre-flight,_

ze-ro ho-ur, nine A. M. _____

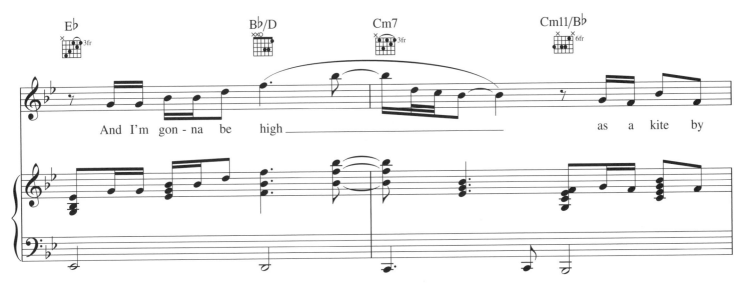

And I'm gon-na be high _____ as a kite by

TINY DANCER

Words and Music by ELTON JOHN
and BERNIE TAUPIN

(1., 3.)Blue - jean ba - by. _____ L. _____ A. la - dy. _____
(2.) Je - sus freaks _____ out in _____ the _____ street _____

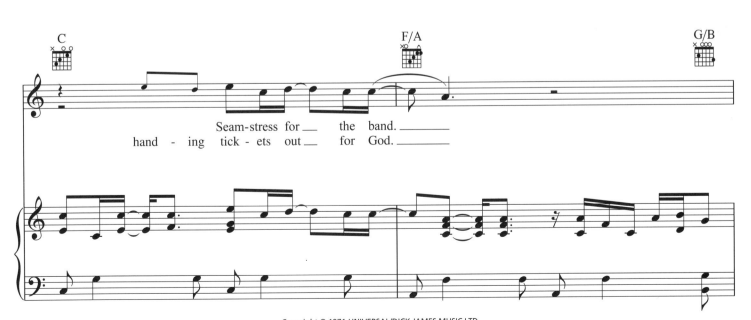

Seam-stress for _____ the band. _____
hand - ing tick-ets out _____ for God. _____

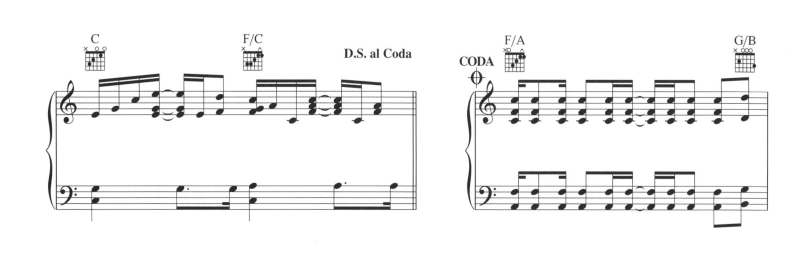

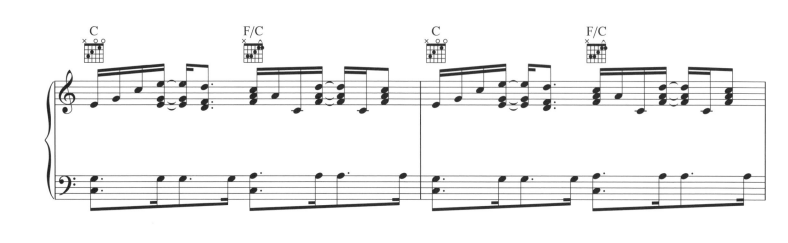

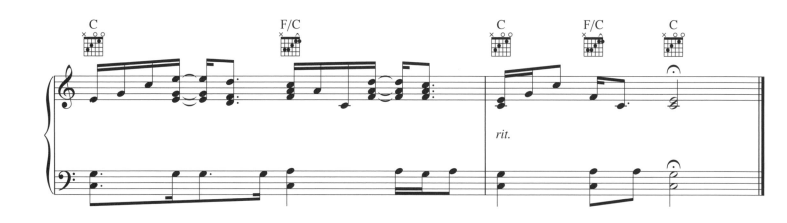

BENNIE AND THE JETS

Words and Music by ELTON JOHN
and BERNIE TAUPIN

Slowly, deliberately

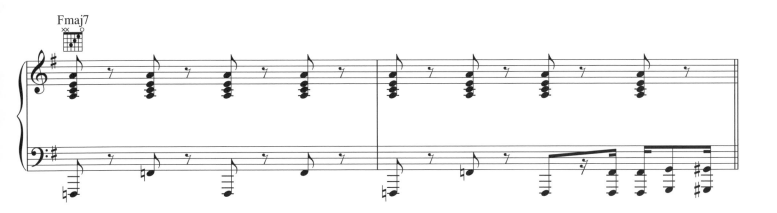

Hey, kids, _ shake _ it loose to-geth-er. The spot - light's hit - ting some-thing that's been known to change the weath-er.
Hey, kids, _ plug _ in - to the faith-less. May - be they're _ blind - ed, but Ben-nie makes them age-less.
Piano solo ad lib.

DANDELIONS

Composed by JAMES NEWTON HOWARD
and CHRIS BACON

THE TIKI TIKI TIKI ROOM

Words and Music by RICHARD M. SHERMAN
and ROBERT B. SHERMAN

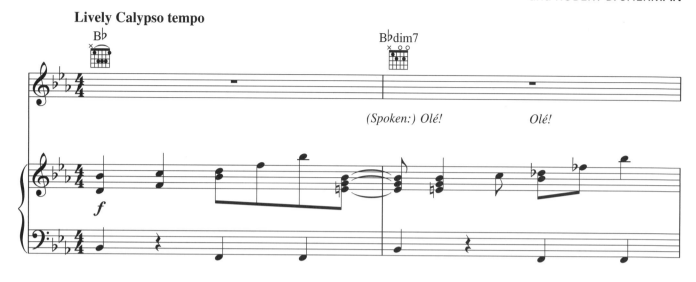

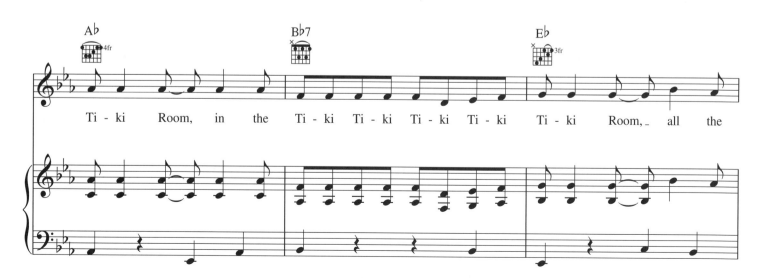